C000241185

# COALVILLE
## A TRIP THROUGH TIME

edited and researched by:
Denis Baker and Steve Duckworth

Acknowledgements:

| | | |
|---|---|---|
| Captions & Research | – | Denis Baker |
| Photography | – | Steve Duckworth |
| Design & Typesetting | – | Steve Duckworth |

Without the financial support of North West Leicestershire District Council this book could not have been produced.

Many thanks to all of the people who have loaned photographs that are featured in this book especially:

Mrs. Donaldson, R.Clarke, J.Edwards, Mrs. Barwick, Leicestershire Museums, B.Hudson, D.Baker, S.M.Duckworth, Mr.E.Deeming, Mrs.Blower, B.Smith, Miss E.M.Smith, B.Chapman, Walter Toon, Ron Bombroff, A.Beniston. Special thanks to Chris Matchett for the loan of so many photographs

© 1994 Coalville Publishing Company Ltd. & Coalville 150 Group.

Photographs    16,17    © Denis Baker – no reproduction without permission.

Photograph    58    © Steve Duckworth – no reproduction without permission.

ISBN 1 872479 20 0

Printed at Alden Press Limited, Oxford and Northampton,Great Britain.

The official launch of this book was sponsored by the Coalville Forum.

*Front Cover* – *This woodcut is a view of Coalville c1840 seen from the railway line beyond Mantle Lane. The church tower in the distance is the tower of Christ Church and the end of the white building in the centre is the "Red House". Over on the right in the trees can just be seen the Ebenezer Baptist Chapel.*

*Back Cover* – *This is a photograph taken from the same viewpoint as the woodcut on the front cover. Much of the detail of the town visible in 1840 is now obscured.*

This book is intended to be the first in a series of Photographic records of the developing Coalville.

It takes the reader on a photographic journey around Coalville to view changes in the townscape over the period of its history. We have also attempted to provide a human dimension by including the names of people living at some locations at various times. It is sad that, with the exception of the woodcut picture on the front cover, technology was not available to record the earliest days but we are fortunate to have the eyewitness account of Coalville in 1830 recorded by Samuel Fisher. His "Reminiscences of Coalville" have been published and are available from Coalville 150 Group.

We hope you will enjoy this evocative record from the past.

Coalville 150 Group was formed in 1982 to celebrate the 150th. anniversary of Coalville in 1983. It continues after the event, publishing books and calendars, mounting exhibitions and maintaining the photographic archive from which the photographs in this book have been drawn. There are currently over 1,000 negatives of the area in this archive.

We would like to thank everyone who has contributed to this archive over the past 12 years by allowing us to copy their photographs. Anyone who has a photograph that they would be prepared to loan for copying please contact; Steve Duckworth on 0530 831270 (after 6pm.).

Regrettably, due to limited resources and time, prints are not generally available to the public. However, researchers and anyone with a strong interest in a particular subject may contact the above number and we will endeavour to fulfil their requests.

The Coalville 150 Group regularly co-operates with other local history groups in the area to present displays in Snibston Discovery Park.

1) Ashby Road, looking towards the town from Ravenstone Turn c1935. The house on the right, Snibstone Cottage, was occupied in 1891 by Samuel Else, a butcher from Coleorton, and his family.

2) A late 1950s photograph of one of the six row of cottages built by Snibston Colliery to house its workers after 1832. Originally "Snibston No. 6 Cottages", it was renamed "Kimberly Row" and in 1881 accommodated 90 persons in the twenty cottages.

3) The rear of "Kimberly Row" shortly before demolition. Shared access to external ashpit closets and coal stores was provided for the following mining families in 1881 - Yearby, Greasley, Reed, Pickering, Locke, Bakewell, Steavenson, Saunders, Hodgetts, Billing, Edwards, Brownlow, Lager, Towers and Kendrick.

4) "Snibston No. 5 Cottages" was renamed "Snibston Buildings West" giving rise to the name "West End" of town. In 1892, its 21 cottages accommodated 109 persons from the Rowell, Yearby, Essex, Maddocks, Moore, Beet, Horrobin, Shaw, Massey, Hodges, Willars, Lycett, Spencer, Siddons, Measures, Lowell, Wyatt, Pickering and Walker families.

5) Ashby Road c1900. Miners from Snibston Colliery, right, could drink at the "Waggon and Horses", "Queens Head" or "Bricklayers Arms". The building furthest away on the left was, in 1891, a beer house run by Samuel Thorpe. The grocer's shop, left, was owned by William and Maria Greasley.

6) Snibston Colliery was sunk by the Company in 1833 under George Stephenson's personal supervision with its own sidings onto the Leicester and Swannington Railway. The Company constructed its own community comprising six rows of cottages and a school house. By 1842 250 men and boys were employed.

7) The Midland Red Garage was constructed in 1925 on the site of the Snibston Rows, Short Row and James Place, the house occupied by James Stephenson, George's brother. By the mid 1930s the garage had nearly 50 buses in operation providing a much valued local service. Photographed at the 1937 coronation celebrations.

8) The "Ebenezer Baptist Church" was inaugurated in 1879 by a group of baptists who separated from the General Baptist Church. They took over a building erected in the early 1830s as Snibston Colliery school, which had been used by the methodists until the 1860s. It provided a centre of excellence for religious music for many years.

9) Ashby Road in 1930 showing Coalville garage erected in 1914 and the "new" post office. The range of shops included the Central Dairy, Dunkley's Drapery, Towers Newsagent, Bentley's Fruiterers, Owen's Saddlery & Sports Equipment and Birmingham Cycles.

10) Coalville town centre c1910. The centre of the town provided wide open spaces and wide streets which accommodated a large open market on Fridays. The area shown includes 6 public houses.

11) The "Snibstone New Inn" at King George V coronation in 1910. The Inn was built in 1836 by Thomas Caldwell, whose family kept it for about 30 years. On the right is part of Deputies (or George's) Row which accommodated the Snibston Mine supervisory managers.

12) The "Green Man", a cast iron urinal erected at the town cross-roads on land provided by W.D.Stableford in 1896, provided a much needed facility for people attending the market which opened in 1879 and the cattle market at the rear of the Red House Inn. Photographed in 1925 when the clock tower was under construction.

13) The "Old Red House" predated Coalville; at the crossing of the old "Long Lane" and "Hugglescote Lane". An early resident of Coalville noted "*known in more than county; indeed anyone even in Derbyshire giving his address as "Red House" indicated the district from which he hailed.*" It was once known as the "Cradle and Coffin".

14) High Street c1910. The houses were set well back to enable the market stalls to be set up along the street. The Stretton's Row on the right was built prior to 1850 and those on the left after 1860 on land left by William Stenson, the founder of Whitwick Colliery.

15) High Street (formerly Station Street) at Queen Victoria's jubilee in 1887. Houses were at this time being converted into shops. On the extreme right is the "Bell Inn" kept by William and Emma Bird; next in "Marshall's Buildings" lived the families of James Bird, Isaac Wardle and John Gardner, a blacksmith. A smithy stood at the rear of this house.

16) High Street in the 1960s prior to demolition to make space for the New Library and Day Centre. Bott's (formerly Stock's) fish and chip shop provided delicious refreshments to several generations of Coalville citizens. The renamed "Blue Bell Inn" on the extreme right was built prior to 1848.

17) The "Blue Bell" and "Fountain" inns stood at the entrance of "Marshalls Row", a terrace of 13 cottages built prior to 1841. The Row provided accommodation in 1891 to 76 persons from the Wilcox, Compton, Joynes, Bird, Egginton, Fairbrother, Brockley, Curtis, Harrison, Tomlin, Hirons, Wardle and White families.

18) The "Fountain Inn" in 1890 was kept by James and Amy Smith. It was probably built in the mid 1840s at the time "Station Row" was built for Midland Railway workers. The row of 7 cottages housed the Stevens, Robinson, Clarke, Edwards, Taylor and Knowles railway families.

19) Station Street in 1905 was by this time well developed. The stationmaster's house is on the right and the imposing building on the left is the Midland Bank. In the range of shops on the left one could buy tobacco, wines, medicines, haberdashery, shoes, jewellery & watches, bread & confectionery, suits, grocery, ironmongery, millinery and toys.

20) The memorial to the fallen of the First World War was erected in the Station Yard wall in 1920. It was removed when the clock tower memorial was erected in 1926.

21) Station Street c1915. The "Stamford and Warrington Arms Hotel" was a Posting House providing horse-drawn carriage transport for travellers arriving at the railway station as well as overnight accommodation. The opening adjacent led to the Rope Works and Rope Walk.

22) Demolition of High Street in 1962 to provide space for the New Broadway Shopping Precinct.

23) Coalville Midland Railway Station c1900. The first station building was erected by the Midland Railway in 1848 but as passenger use developed the station was enlarged in 1865 and again to the building shown in 1894. Passenger services ended on the 7th. September 1964.

24) The crossing and signal box c1910. The footbridge was built in 1851 to cope with the large volume of rail traffic, a signal box was placed at ground level in 1856. With the erection of the new station the box was elevated in 1907 providing better sight lines. The Railway Hotel was a ticket office to the original Leicester and Swannington in 1832.

25) Hotel Street c1900. The low level signal box can be seen at the level crossing. The shops on the right were Wortley – shoemaker, Baker – newsagent, Conniffe – tailor, Hawthorne – tailor, Tivey – sweets and Gough – fruiterer. On the left can be seen the new post office, Tebbit – saddler, Smith – grocer and Biddles & Tyler – cycles.

26) F.Kemp's High Class Grocery was built into the Cave Adullam chapel. This was a Strict Baptist Chapel sponsored by William Stenson in 1852 opposite the General Baptist Chapel. It flourished for some time until after 1907 when it was sold for commercial premises. Photo c1950.

27) London Road Baptist Chapel (Top Baptist) c1920. The original chapel was erected on land given by the Whitwick Colliery in 1835 under the supervision of Hugglescote Baptist Chapel. It was separated from Hugglescote in 1856 and enlarged in 1861 when a new day school "The British School" was erected. it had a very high reputation in the area.

28) Whitwick Road leading to Whitwick Colliery c1920. Just beyond the wall was the railway siding which originally connected the Colliery to the Leicester and Swannington Railway in 1832. Long Lane Colliery was sunk in 1824 by William Stenson who initiated the building of the railway.

29) Club Row c1930. This row was built to house some of the early miners who came into Coalville in the 1830s. They were built by the "Coalville Building Society" and called the "Club Houses". By 1880 they were known as Coalville Place but by 1910 were renamed Club Row. The nearest ones belonged to the Colliery.

30) Architect's drawing of Christ Church, its parsonage and national day school. Erected 1836-38 on a site donated by William Stenson. It was initially under the patronage of Rev. Minton of Durham. The gravestone of James Stephenson is preserved in the church, there is also a memorial plaque to the miners who died in the Whitwick Colliery disaster.

31) London Road c1920. The houses on London Road were built primarily for the middle class professional and tradespeople through the early history of the town.

32) Coalville Park c1905. This land was purchased in the 1880s by the Coalville Athletic Club who raised £3000 by organising a grand sports each year which attracted large crowds. The land was gifted to the local council in 1899. The Park was opened in May 1900.

33) London Road c1950 showing one of the farms which existed on Long Lane prior to the arrival of the railway. Known as Moores farm it soon lost land to the developers. On the right can be seen Coalville East Post Office, Wortley's – shoe repairers, College's – gents hairdressers, and Surman's Butchers.

34) A meeting of the Quorn Hunt on Leicester Road at the Fox & Goose in 1895. One of the original row of 5 cottages occupied in 1891 had been demolished to provide space for the single storey extension. Fox & Goose cottages were built prior to 1841.

35) The Fox & Goose Hotel c1910, kept by William Butler, replace the earlier and much smaller beer house kept by a Thomas Smith in 1841. The sign to the London & North Western Railway Station at the end of Ivy Street (now Charnwood Street) can also be seen.

36) Coalville East Station c1950 then abandoned, serviced the Charnwood Forest Railway which connected the town with Loughborough in 1883. The single track lined passed through stations at Whitwick, Thringstone, Grace Dieu and Shepshed and had sidings to local granite companies. It didn't prove a financial success.

37) London Road c1920. This area, including Bardon Road, was developed early this century in open fields beyond the Fox & Goose.

38) St. Dorothy's convent c1920. This house ("The Scotlands") was built by O.Lindley for John Puxley White, the managing director of the South Leicester Colliery Company in 1875 and was purchased from the convent by Dr. Jamie, a surgeon at the Leicester Infirmary. It was demolished in 1938 providing space for the new housing.

39) Central Road from the entrance to Bridge Road c1916. The photograph shows one of the many parades organised to raise funds for a Coalville Hospital. Passing the "Half Way Inn". Central Road was then called Hugglescote Lane.

40) Entrance to Bridge Road c1920. Bridge Road New Council School was opened in 1908 after a long campaign for secondary provision. It provided a sound education including vocational studies for 600 children and opportunities for evening class study.

41) Belvoir Road c1920 showing the old police station and on the left in the distance Whiteleys, a farm which predates the town by at least 100 years. The Vaughan Street, James Street area of the town was developed by James Gutteridge in the 1880s.

42) Whiteleys Farm. c1890. It was mentioned by Samuel Fisher as one of the buildings which considerably predates Coalville and is thought to have been built c1750. It stood at the junction of Belvoir Road and James Street (the present car park).

Belvoir Road, Coalville.

43) Belvoir Road c1940. On the left Candy's cycle shop and on the right the Weslyan Methodist Chapel built in 1881 in an area known as Whiteleys. The adjacent street was for many years known as Chapel Street. The scene, very much as it is today, includes Mr. Ellis delivering milk.

Marlboro' Square, Coalville.

44) Coalville Working Men's Co-operative Society in Marlborough Square c1900. The original shop in Melbourne Street opened in 1882. The building at the far end of the square, Wilkin's Farm, was demolished to make way for further expansion in 1916.

Belvoir Road, Coalville.

45) The Co-op clock was a major social landmark in the town, denoting the end of the "Monkey Walk". On the right the Co-operative drapery, boots, tailoring and outfitting, mantle and millinery departments, built by Griffin Brothers to a design by T.I.McCarthy, was opened in 1916.

46) A public meeting at Queen Victoria's golden Jubilee, 1887, in the Newmarket, an area at present occupied by Marlborough Square, Belvoir Road and Jackson Street. The cottages on the right were called "Bug and Flea Row". The Primitive Methodist Chapel and school can be seen at the top centre.

47) Lloyds bank built on the Newmarket in 1905. Opposite stood the Public Hall built to hold 500 persons in 1876. Next was the Engineers Arms kept by Henry Starkey. Taylor's (Bug and Flea) Row had been improved and converted into shops for: Morris – toys & pictures, Rawlings – furniture, Wood – provisions and Hickling – confectionery.

48) Coalville Electric Theatre (c1910) was opened by Mr. Johnson about 1910 by converting the old Public Hall into a cinematograph centre. It was later developed as the "Grand Cinema" one of the three operated later by Mr. C.K.Deeming.

49) A parade marking Queen Victoria's Diamond Jubilee marches into the New Market in 1897. Two houses in Bug and Flea row had been converted into the shops of W.Morris – picture framer and Hickling – confectioner.

50) 24 houses were built in Jackson Street in 1899 and in 1903 the Primitive Methodists moved from Hugglescote Lane (Belvoir Road) to their new chapel in Marlborough Square. Opposite was built the Olympia Theatre. The development of the far end took place from 1905. (Photograph c1935)

51) Olympia Skating rink, opened in 1909 by Coalville Olympia Limited., a local company formed to provide entertainments by local businessmen G.H.Coleman, A.B.Moss, C.E.Crane, T.I.McCarthy, F.J.Bayliss, A.Wilkins and G.Gutteridge. Later it was sold to Mr.Deeming in the 1920s who eventually built the Regal Cinema on the site.

52) Coleman and Sons opened a considerable ironmongery and petroleum business in the New Market in 1909. It provided ironmongery to the local community as well as farm equipment. Photo c1920.

53) Coleman's Corner and Oliver's Crossing c1915. The four shops on the left were in a building converted from the old Primitive Methodist Chapel in 1904 by the new owner Mr.P.Greasly, a tobacconist. On the right was Sansomes – drapers and milliners.

Belvoir Road, Coalville.

E.38448

54) Belvoir Road (Hugglescote Lane) c1900. The houses on the right were built in the 1860s and converted later into shops as business developed. The shops on the left were infilled piecemeal from 1877.

55) Pickworth's drapery was the first shop to open on the west side of Hugglescote Lane as early as 1877. They also had a branch at Ibstock. Their address was Atlas House.

56) Demolition of part of the east side of Belvoir Road to provide access for the New Broadway Precinct on the Central Field. The field covered an area of a former brickyard. There was a Rope Walk behind the buildings in the upper part of the photograph.

57) Belvoir Road looking south c1915 shows the extent of the conversion into shops. On the left was: Roughton – chemist, Myatt – cycles, Frampton – draper, Moss – jeweller, Ogden – herbalist, Nash – fancy goods. On the right was Huson – butcher, Hiltons – shoes, Penny Bazaar, Pickworths – drapers, Albrighton – butchers and Betts – grocers.

58) View of Belvoir Road from the top of the Clock Tower in 1978.

59) Coalville Clock Tower and Memorial Square c1935. The cottages on the right hand side of Memorial Square were built by W.D.Stableford to house many workers who came from the Black Country to work in the waggon works.

The Roundabout, Coalville

60) Coalville centre traffic island c1955 showing the new post office and covered market which attracted people from a wide area.